# Claude Monet
## The Painter Who Stopped the Trains

By P. I. Maltbie
Illustrated by Jos. A. Smith

Abrams Books for Young Readers
New York

*P*apa . . . *look!* The train is coming . . ."

Claude Monet turned away from his painting to see his nine-year-old son, Jean, waving at a train as it rushed across the French countryside.

"Hello-o-o," Jean cried out as he waved his handkerchief. "Say 'bonjour' to all the people in Paris."

The year was 1876, and trains were the fastest, most modern form of transportation. Just to see one rushing by was thrilling to most people, and especially to Jean. A few minutes after it disappeared from sight, the train he was watching would be arriving in Paris. After that, it would be racing off to another town.

As Claude watched his son's delight, he wished that his paintings could produce the same sense of energy and excitement as the speeding train. But it seemed as if his paintings just made people angry, especially the art critics.

"Those *Impressionists!*" the critics sniffed. "Their paintings look as if the paint was fired from a gun. And that Monet is the worst of the lot."

Claude didn't like to be called an Impressionist. But that's what the art critics called him and his artist friends after an exhibition of their paintings in 1874. One of his paintings was a seascape, which he called *Impression, Sunrise.* It was painted with bright strokes of color, something the popular artists of that time did not do. They painted grandly but precisely or realistically. Claude had also painted an ordinary scene rather than an event from history or from a myth or legend.

Furthermore, instead of sitting in a dark studio, Claude had painted out of doors to capture a moment of time and the effect of sunlight on his subject. The name Impressionist became a popular way to poke fun at this new style of painting.

*Well,* Claude thought, *I have always gone my own way when it comes to painting. I am not going to change now.*

"It's time for lunch," Claude said as he checked his watch. "We will return later when the light has changed."

Back home, his wife, Camille, was waiting. With her were two of Claude's friends from Paris—the artists Pierre-Auguste Renoir and Gustave Caillebotte.

"We've come to have lunch with you," they said.

As they ate, Pierre-Auguste and Gustave talked about an exhibition of their paintings, which they were planning to hold in Paris the following April.

"We really want you to join us," Pierre-Auguste said. "After all, it wouldn't be an exhibit of the *Impressionists* without you."

Pierre-Auguste liked to tease Claude by calling him an Impressionist. But since they were such good friends, Claude did not mind it.

"And I'll pay to rent the exhibition hall," Gustave added. "So any money you and Pierre-Auguste and the others make from selling your paintings will be pure profit."

Gustave was different from the other Impressionists. He came from a wealthy family, so he didn't have to sell his paintings in order to live. Instead, he used his generous allowance to buy his friends' paintings and to help them in other ways. His offer to rent the hall would be a great help to Claude, Pierre-Auguste, and their friends.

After lunch, the three artists relaxed in Claude's beautiful garden. While they talked of the exhibition, Jean played nearby with his toy train.

"*Woossshhhttt. Ggrrrumm.*" Jean made train noises. Stuffing a bit of cotton into the smokestack made the train look as if it were giving off a cloud of steam as it rumbled through the grass.

"Maybe you could show some of the paintings you are working on now," Gustave said.

"Or maybe you'll have something new," Pierre-Auguste suggested.

"Perhaps," Claude agreed. But what could he paint that would not anger the critics? If they did not like his work, his paintings would not sell.

After his friends left, Claude continued to watch Jean play with his toy train. The wisp of cotton Jean had stuffed into the smokestack reminded Claude of the fog and mist he had captured in his seascape painting. Suddenly, he had an idea: *Trains! I'll show them with their engines just starting. With smoke from the engines so thick, the critics will hardly see a thing. If they don't think fog at the seashore is a proper subject for my paintings, I'll give them a modern city scene. A view of Paris today, but filled with steam and smoke! It'll be a dream world, but a modern dream world.*

Instead of one painting, Claude decided he would create several paintings. Each one would show a different moment in time and how the train's steam and smoke affected the scene.

But Claude did not start working on his idea right away. He had to find a train station where the effects of sunlight on smoke and steam would produce the mood he wanted to capture in his paintings. He would also need a studio close by where he could live while he worked on his paintings.

In January 1877, after visiting each train station in Paris, Claude decided that the Saint-Lazare was just what he wanted. Nearby was an apartment he could use for his studio. Now he would put the most important part of his plan in motion.

The artist put on his best clothes, which he had brought from home: his best suit, a fine top hat, a linen shirt, and a handsome silk tie. Cuff buttons flashed at his wrists, and a gold-headed walking stick twirled between his fingertips.

Looking like a wealthy gentleman, Claude strolled from his studio apartment to the office of the director of the Saint-Lazare station.

"I have some very important business to discuss with Monsieur the Director," he said as he handed the clerk his card—

## *Claude Monet*
### PAINTER

The clerk looked at the card, and then looked at Claude. Such an elegant gentleman had to be very important indeed! So, without asking any questions, the clerk led Claude into the director's office.

"How do you do," Claude said. "I am the artist Claude Monet."

Immediately, Claude could see that the director didn't have any idea who he was, but did not have the courage to say so.

"For some time, I have wanted to paint a series of pictures of a train station . . . to show the world how Paris is moving into the modern age," he continued. "And after visiting all the stations in Paris, I have chosen yours as my model. I think it has much more character than any of the others."

The director stammered, "Th-thank you, Monsieur . . . Monet."

"I would like to set up my easel on the platform so I can capture the engines pulling into the station and preparing to leave. I want plenty of smoke and steam. Will that be a problem?"

"Oh no, monsieur, I would be honored. You can rely on me and my staff to help you in any way we can."

"And it may be necessary to delay the trains' departures," Claude added, "so that I may completely capture the effect of light through the steam and smoke."

"Of course, monsieur. It can be arranged."

For the next few months, Claude was seen on the platform of the Saint-Lazare station, painting. While the director and a few of his assistants stood by in respectful silence, Claude worked. He showed the trains leaving and arriving from different angles, the bustling of the crowds, and the changes of color and light. As the platform rumbled and shook under him like an earthquake, Claude remembered Jean's excitement and worked to put it in his paintings.

He also ignored the sensation he was creating.

"Who does he think he is?" several angry passengers sputtered. "Holding up the trains so he may paint them!"

"This is an outrage!" another passenger told the director. "I have an important business meeting in Rouen . . . I cannot be kept waiting for the train to leave."

But the director just shrugged. What did it matter if a few passengers were angered by the delay? His station was going to be captured in a series of masterpieces by Claude Monet!

And when Claude wanted to show the way light played on the gusts of steam, the director was ready to help. He had the train's engineer shovel coal into the furnace so thick clouds of white and gray would fill the station.

Claude worked on more than one picture at a time, changing the canvas when the light shifted. When he was finished for the day, he would pack up his painting supplies and his canvases and return to his studio.

By April 1877, the paintings were finished and ready for the exhibition. Claude was pleased to show Camille and Jean that his paintings had their own room. One picture had even been chosen to hang by the entrance of the show.

"See, Jean? I have captured your speeding locomotives for all time," he said.

"You have truly shown how art can reflect modern city life," Pierre-Auguste told Claude.

"Instead of retelling stuffy old legends and stories from history," Gustave added.

The public's response to the exhibition of 1877 was more excitement than mockery. It became an event that many people discussed and visited. Émile Zola, one of the most famous authors and art critics at that time, wrote a positive review of the exhibition:

"Monsieur Claude Monet has the most distinctive personality of the Impressionists. He has exhibited some superb interiors of the railway station. You can hear the trains rumbling in, see the smoke billow up under the huge roofs . . . That is where painting is today . . . Our artists have to find the poetry in the train stations, the way their fathers found poetry in forests and rivers."

When the exhibition was over, an important art dealer offered to buy the series of Saint-Lazare paintings. Now Claude would have the money he needed to work on other paintings.

Those would be painted back home, however, in his colorful gardens and in the countryside of Argenteuil. Claude and his family returned to the Saint-Lazare station, climbed on the train headed north, and returned home.

*Portrait of Claude Monet*, by Pierre-Auguste Renoir. 1875. Oil on canvas. Musée d'Orsay, Paris, France.

*Portrait of Jean Monet*, at age thirteen, by Claude Monet. 1880. Oil on canvas. Musée Marmottan, Paris, France.

# Author's Note

When trains first started rumbling over the French countryside in the 1830s and 1840s, many people predicted the end of a peaceful world because of the soot and noise that would come with the railroads. But trains allowed people to travel easily and economically between Paris and the surrounding towns.

From 1871 to 1878, Claude Monet (1840–1926), his wife, Camille, and their son, Jean, lived in the village of Argenteuil, just six miles north of Paris. The colorful landscapes around Argenteuil inspired many of Monet's paintings. It was also close enough to Paris for him to make frequent train trips to visit other artists and to sell his paintings.

In April 1874, Monet and his friends showed their paintings in what would be later called the first Impressionist exhibition. Their paintings caused a sensation because they were painted outdoors or they captured places the average person would know. The Impressionists used bright colors, and their brushstrokes could be seen easily, a technique not used by the popular, accepted artists of the day.

In January 1877, Monet decided to concentrate on city scenes in and around Paris. The idea was very new and controversial. Most people preferred to buy paintings of scenes from ancient legends, historical events, or stories from the Bible. Since train travel was the most modern form of transportation, Monet decided to paint a series of pictures of the Gare Saint-Lazare at different times of the day. (*Gare* is French for "train station.")

But to do this, Monet needed to get permission from the director of the train station so he could set up his easel and paint on the busy platforms. According to Pierre-Auguste Renoir, who told the story many times to his sons (and preserved it for history), Monet wore his best suit of clothes when he visited the director. From January to March of 1877, Monet painted the Gare Saint-Lazare series, which was quickly purchased by one of the most important art dealers of the time, Paul Durand-Ruel.

Monet enjoyed the challenge of trying to capture the impressions of light on steam and smoke. The different effects of the changing light as it poured through the station's glass panes overhead proved to Monet that he had found the proper subject for his paintings. While passengers rushed all around the station to get off or on the trains, he worked quickly. The finishing touches would be added when he returned to his nearby studio.

Monet was so pleased with how well these paintings turned out that he continued to paint several pictures of a single subject . . . as he did in his series of grain stacks, scenes of Venice, scenes of London, the Rouen Cathedral, poplar trees, seascapes and riverscapes, and the wonderful gardens and lily pond around his final home in Giverny. Although most of Monet's later paintings would focus on outdoor scenes, he would continue to depend on the trains of the Gare Saint-Lazare as a way to travel to all his favorite painting locations.

Most of the events in my story are based on true events, and all the people I mention were involved in Monet's life at this time. The scene in which Jean Monet (1867–1914) is playing with his toy train came from my imagination. Jean was nine at the time, just the age to be fascinated by trains; and, like many children, he would have had a toy train made of iron or tin. Since Monet had included portraits of Jean in his landscapes of the 1870s, I decided to have Jean inspire his father to create his first series of paintings.

## Then and Now

The Gare Saint-Lazare was the first train station in Paris. The first building was constructed in 1837. Additions followed in 1841–43 and 1851–53. Trains leaving the Paris station would take their passengers as far as Normandy. Today, thanks to the English Channel Tunnel (or "Chunnel"), trains can carry their passengers all the way to Great Britain.

The Gare Saint-Lazare as it appeared in the late nineteenth century.

*The Gare Saint-Lazare: Arrival of a Train,* by Claude Monet. 1877. Oil on canvas. Harvard Art Museum.

# Museums

Some of Claude Monet's paintings can be found in these museums.

(Entries in boldface indicate museums that house some of Monet's Gare Saint-Lazare paintings.)

## United States

Albright-Knox Gallery, Buffalo, N.Y.

Allen Memorial Art Museum, Oberlin, Ohio

**Art Institute of Chicago, Chicago, Ill.**

Baltimore Museum of Art, Baltimore, Md.

Birmingham Museum of Art, Birmingham, Ala.

Brooklyn Museum, Brooklyn, N.Y.

California Palace of the Legion of Honor, San Francisco, Calif.

Carnegie Museum of Art, Pittsburgh, Penn.

Cleveland Museum of Art, Cleveland, Ohio

Columbus Museum of Art, Columbus, Ohio

Currier Gallery of Art, Manchester, N.H.

Dallas Museum of Art, Dallas Tex.

Dayton Art Institute, Dayton, Ohio

Denver Art Museum, Denver, Colo.

Detroit Institute of Arts, Detroit, Mich.

**Harvard Art Museum, Cambridge, Mass.**

Getty Center, Los Angeles, Calif.

Harn Museum of Art, Gainesville, Fla.

Hill-Stead Museum, Farmington, Conn.

Honolulu Academy of Art, Honolulu, Hawaii

Indianapolis Museum of Art, Indianapolis, Ind.

Kimball Art Museum, Fort Worth, Tex.

Kreeger Museum, Washington, D.C.

Los Angeles County Museum of Art, Los Angeles, Calif.

Marion Koogler McNay Art Museum, San Antonio, Tex.

Mead Art Museum, Amherst, Mass.

Metropolitan Museum of Art, New York, N.Y.

Milwaukee Art Museum, Milwaukee, Wis.

Minneapolis Institute of Arts, Minneapolis, Minn.

Museum of Art, New Orleans, La.

Museum of Fine Arts, Boston, Mass.

Museum of Fine Arts, Houston, Tex.

Museum of Fine Arts, Saint Petersburg, Fla.

Michele & Donald D'Amour Museum of Fine Arts, Springfield, Mass.

Museum of Modern Art, New York, N.Y.

National Gallery of Art, Washington, D.C.

Nelson-Atkins Museum of Art, Kansas City, Mo.

North Carolina Museum of Art, Raleigh, N.C.

Norton Simon Museum, Pasadena, Calif.

Philadelphia Museum of Art, Philadelphia, Penn.

Phoenix Art Museum, Phoenix, Ariz.

Portland Art Museum, Portland, Ore.

Princeton University Art Museum, Princeton, N.J.

Saint Louis Art Museum, Saint Louis, Mo.

San Diego Museum of Art, San Diego, Calif.

Santa Barbara Museum of Art, Santa Barbara, Calif.

Shelburne Museum, Shelburne, Vt.

Smith College Museum, Northampton, Mass.

Speed Art Museum, Louisville, Ky.

Sterling and Francine Clark Art Institute, Williamstown, Mass.

Toledo Museum of Art, Toledo, Ohio

University of Michigan Museum of Art, Ann Arbor, Mich.

Virginia Museum of Fine Art, Richmond, Va.

Wadsworth Atheneum Museum of Art, Hartford, Conn.

Walters Art Gallery, Baltimore, Md.

Worcester Art Museum, Worcester, Mass.

## Canada

National Gallery of Canada, Ottawa

Musée des Beaux-Arts, Montreal

Art Gallery of Ontario, Toronto

# Select Bibliography

If you are interested in learning more about Claude Monet, here are some other books you might like.

Anholt, Laurence. *The Magical Garden of Claude Monet*. New York: Barron's Educational Series, 2007.

Carvalho de Magalhaes, Roberto. *Claude Monet* (Great Artists). New York: Enchanted Lion, 2005.

Connolly, Sean. *The Life and Work of Claude Monet*. Chicago: Heinemann-Raintree, 2005.

Hodge, Susie. *Claude Monet* (Artists in Their Time). London: Franklin Watts, 2002.

Klein, Adam G. *Claude Monet* (Great Artists). Edina, MN: ADBO Publishing Co., 2007.

LeTord, Bijou. *A Blue Butterfly*. New York: Doubleday, 1995.

Malam, John. *Claude Monet* (Tell Me About). Minneapolis: Carolrhoda Books, Inc., 1997.

Muhlberger, Richard. *What Makes a Monet a Monet?* New York: Viking Juvenile, 2002.

Renoir, Jean. *Renoir, My Father*. Translated by Randolph Weaver and Dorothy Weaver. New York: New York Review of Books, 2001.

Sabbath, Carol. *Monet and the Impressionists for Kids: Their Lives and Ideas, 21 Activities* (For Kids Series). Chicago: Chicago Review Press, 2002.

Waldron, Ann. *Claude Monet. First Impressions*. New York: Harry N. Abrams, 1991.

Welton, Jude. *Eyewitness Art: Monet*. NY: Dorling Kindersley, 1999.

Wilson-Bareau. *Manet, Monet and the Gare St. Lazare*. New Haven, CT: Yale University Press, 1998.

# Index

Page numbers in italics refer to illustrations.

Argenteuil (France), 26, 28
art critics, 3–4, 10, 25
art dealers, 25, 28

Caillebotte, Gustave, 8–10, 22
"Chunnel" (English Channel Tunnel), 29

Durand-Ruel, Paul, 28

English Channel Tunnel, 29

"first Impressionist exhibition" (1874), 4, 28

*Gare Saint-Lazare: Arrival of a Train, The* (Monet), *29*
Gare Saint-Lazare paintings (Monet), *29*
    exhibition of (1877), 22–25
    painting process for, 17–21, 28–29
Gare Saint-Lazare (Paris)
    photograph of, *29*
    station director, 14–19, 21, 28
*Gare* ("train station"), 28

*Impression, Sunrise* (Monet), 4
Impressionist art exhibition (1874), 4, 28
Impressionist art exhibition (1877), 8–10, 22–25
Impressionist art style, 4–5, 28

Monet, Camille, 8, 22, 28
Monet, Claude
    and art critics, 3–4, 10, 25
    and art dealers, 28
    and the term "Impressionist", 9
    homes of, 26, 28, 29
    studio of, 12, 21
    subjects for paintings by, 4, 11, 28, 29
Monet, Jean, 3, 10–11, 22, 28, 29

Renoir, Pierre-Auguste, 8–10, 22, 28

toy trains, 10, 11, 29
train station paintings (Monet), 11–12
    *See also* Gare Saint-Lazare paintings (Monet)
train stations. *See* Gare Saint-Lazare (Paris)
train travel, in France, 3, 28, 29

Zola, Émile, 25

For Jan and George Saade—without their friendship and staunch advocacy, this story could not have been written.

—P. I. M.

For Julie Saab and fellow artist David Gothard, two very special people, for your generosity, friendship, and kindness. You should be cloned.

—J. A. S.

## Artist's Note

I had to first decide the look of the pictures. I could use loose, Impressionist-like brushwork, or treat them more realistically. I chose not to try to imitate Monet's masterful brushwork. This would have made any examples of his paintings feel like they were merely copies of his world rather than brilliant new visions. I did not want to underplay how much of a departure his vision was. I was able to use archival photographs and a number of books as reference material, among them *The Impressionists by Themselves*, edited by Michael Howard; *Claude Monet: The Color of Time*, by Virginia Spate; *Monet*, by Christopher Heinrich; and *Monet: A Retrospective*, edited by Chas. F. Stuckey. For fashion of the period, I found particularly helpful *Degas*, by Jean Sutherland Boggs, and *20,000 Years of Fashion: The History of Costume and Personal Adornment*, by François Boucher. For the trains, *Steam Trains*, by Bill Hayes, was very useful. (Although it and several other books on steam trains were of minimal to no help dealing with Monet's lack of detail—he was, after all, quoted as saying, "For me, the subject is of secondary importance: I want to convey what is alive between me and the subject.")

My illustrations were done on an Arches 140 lb. 18" x 24" hot-press watercolor block. I first did a series of rough pencil drawings to experiment with different compositions. When I knew what I wanted, I sketched the drawings lightly in pencil or watercolor pencil. I then worked with transparent watercolor. In some of the illustrations, I put in final color or detail touches with watercolor pencils. I built up the illustrations in a series of transparent layers. I was working in the same size as the printed book because I did not want the illustrations to look more refined by being reduced from larger paintings for printing. This gave the pictures a slightly "rougher" look, to let my act of painting show. I worked on the more complicated pictures for four or five days each.

Just as Monet had fun at the train station with the stationmaster and passengers, I decided to have my fun as well. In one of the last illustrations, showing Monet and his family and friends looking at his painting at the exhibition, I added Mary Cassatt, in the far left background, her back to us, looking at her own painting of a girl sitting in a blue chair. I also included a self-portrait. In the illustration where Monet is looking at the Gare Saint-Lazare, I am wearing a high top hat, entering the picture from the far left.

## Image Credits

Renoir, Pierre-Auguste (1841–1919). *Portrait of Claude Monet*, 1875. Oil on canvas, 85 x 60.5 cm. Inv. RF3666. Photo: Jean-Gilles Berizzi. Photo Credit: Réunion des Musées Nationaux/Art Resource, NY. Musée d'Orsay, Paris, France.
*Portrait of Jean Monet*, at age 13, by Claude Monet. 1880. Oil on canvas. Musée Marmottan, Paris, France.
*The Gare Saint-Lazare: Arrival of a Train*, Claude Monet. 1877. Oil on canvas. 80.33 x 98.11 cm. Harvard Art Museum.

Library of Congress Cataloging-in-Publication Data
Maltbie, P. I.
Claude Monet : the painter who stopped the trains / by P.I. Maltbie ; illustrated by Jos. A. Smith.
p. cm.
Includes bibliographical references and index.
ISBN 978-0-8109-8961-0 (alk. paper)
1. Monet, Claude, 1840–1926—Juvenile literature. 2. Painters—France—Biography—Juvenile literature. I. Monet, Claude, 1840–1926. II. Smith, Joseph A. (Joseph Anthony), 1936– III. Title.
ND553.M7M2865 2010
759.4—dc22
[B]
2009039459

Text copyright © 2010 P. I. Maltbie
Illustrations copyright © 2010 Jos. A. Smith
Book design by Maria T. Middleton

Printed and bound in China
10 9 8 7 6 5 4 3 2 1

Abrams Books for Young Readers are available at special discounts when purchased in quantity for premiums and promotions as well as fundraising or educational use. Special editions can also be created to specification. For details, contact specialmarkets@abramsbooks.com or the address below.

ABRAMS
THE ART OF BOOKS SINCE 1949
115 West 18th Street
New York, NY 10011
www.abramsbooks.com